Thirty-One Days of Prayers for My Grandchildren

by
Opal Ashenbrenner
(Granapple)

PublishAmerica
Baltimore

First printing

ISBN: 1-4137-4317-X
PUBLISHED BY PUBLISHAMERICA, LLLP
www.publishamerica.com
Baltimore

Printed in the United States of America

Dedication

To my wonderful husband, Don, with whom I have found true happiness. Thank you for your unconditional love, encouragement and support in everything I do.

And

To my children, Susie and Jack Johnson, Paul and Terri Koonce who's parenting skills produced my wonderful grandchildren. They all have brought so much joy and happiness to my life.

Acknowledgments

I am so thankful to God for allowing me the awesome experience of being a grandparent. From the day each of my grandchildren was born, I began praying that God would watch over their lives and use them for His glory. He has abundantly answered my prayers. Brian, now 22 years is a senior at Oklahoma Baptist University; Jordan is 21 years and a Junior at Texas Tech, and Brooke just completed her freshman year at West Texas A&M and is now experiencing the "real world." Kelly is 17 years and a senior at Bartlesville High School, Bartlesville, Oklahoma. They all have loving, caring hearts and God has blessed me greatly as I have seen His marvelous works in their lives, not only when they were four or five years old, but even more so now as they continue to serve their Lord as young adults. Their energy and joy for living inspires me every day.

Along with my own grandchildren, my marriage to Don Ashenbrenner several years ago brought two more wonderful additions to my grandmother experience. Greg and Holly Loeffler have graciously allowed me to become their "Granapple" as well. Even though Greg and Holly came into my life long after the original manuscript was written, they are truly the "apples of my eye."

Special Thanks

A very special thank you goes to good friends, Judy McKee and Sue Clark whose friendship and critiquing skills were invaluable in putting this together. You are appreciated more than you will ever know. I love you both.

Day One

Keep me as the apple of the eye, hide me under the shadow of thy wings.
Psalm 17:8 KJV

Apples are important in our house. My favorite food in the entire world is apples. I love apple butter and apple juice. I have apple dishes, drinking glasses, necklaces, and numerous other apple things in my house. I just love apples. My grandchildren always knew when they came to my house they would get an apple for a treat instead of candy. The grandchildren even call me "Granapple." My name is Opal, so when Brian my first grandson began to talk, the Grandma Opal became "Granapple." That name was quickly picked up as the other grandchildren came along.

As they grew, all their friends began calling me Granapple also. I love being called Granapple by my grandchildren and I love telling each of them that they are the apple of my eye. I had to explain to each one of them as they grew old enough to understand that being the apple of my eye meant that they were doing the things that pleased me. Just as they are the apples of my eye, I want to live my life so that my heavenly Father can say of me as He did of David, "You are the apple of my eye."

"Oh God, thank You for your protection every day and for keeping the apples of my eye safe. Father, keep them in Your perfect care and may they always live for You. More important than being the apple of my eye, I want You to be able to say of them as You did of David, 'You are the apple of My Eye."

Jordan Johnson

Day Two

For God so loved the world, that He gave His only begotten Son, that whosoever believeth in Him should not perish, but have everlasting life. John 3:16 KJV

Having lived on a farm in the Oklahoma panhandle all his life, five-year-old Jordan loved the outdoors. Most any day you could find Jordan with Sissy, his little toy Dachshund, at his heels, exploring things that little boys and dogs explore on a working farm. One day while walking around the farm, Jordan heard the rattle that he recognized as the sound of a deadly rattlesnake. Sissy, sensing the danger to her beloved Jordan, positioned herself between him and the rattlesnake. One strike of the rattlesnake and the little dog was dead. She had given her life so that the one she loved could live.

What a parallel in our lives! Jesus Christ has given His life so that we, whom He loves, can live. It took Jordan a long time to get over losing his little dog; however, the incident did help him to understand more fully the sacrifice Christ made for each of us.

"O Lord, may we never forget how much You love us and that You gave Your only son to die in our place so that we may have eternal life. May Jordan and my other grandchildren always remember the sacrifice You made for us."

Day Three

I will bless the Lord at all times: his praise shall continually be in my mouth. Psalm 34:1KJV

I was having Sunday dinner with my son and his family when four-year old Brian asked to say the blessing. He prayed, "God bless Granapple, Mommie, and Brother Paul." When he finished praying I asked if he always called his daddy Brother Paul. "No," Brian replied, "just on Sundays." It made sense to him. He was daddy all week, but on Sundays he was pastor of the church.

Sunday was a very special day to Brian as it should be to all of us. We cannot live any way we please all week and then go to church on Sunday and tell God how much we love Him. How thankful I am that God shows us how much He loves us every day of the week and not just on Sundays. We are so blessed with the benefits of God's love. I want my grandchildren to discover what a high privilege it is to praise God and learn to live a life of worship and praise; not just on Sundays but every day of the week in every situation.

"Father, help me to lead my grandchildren to cultivate a lifestyle of praise and worship as they serve You, our Lord and Master. Help them to discover that praising You is an exciting adventure that yields deeper knowledge of how wonderful, loving and forgiving You are. May their lives reflect You every day of the week."

Day Four

...and at that time thy people shall be delivered, every one that shall be found written in the book. Daniel 12:1c KJV

One day as I was writing in my journal I noticed four-year-old Brooke becoming very interested in what I was doing. She finally asked, "What are you doing, Granapple?"

"I'm writing in my journal," I replied.

"What's a journal?" was her next question.

I very carefully explained that in that book I recorded all the cute things she and her brother did or said so that in years to come I could look back and remember how precious they were.

Sometime later I overheard Brooke talking to her brother. "Jordan," she said very seriously, "we'd better get to doing something cute so our names will be in Granapple's book."

She needn't have worried. Their names will always be in my book and in my heart. The important thing is whether their names are written in the *Lamb's Book of Life*. My prayer for all four of my precious grandchildren is that someday they will accept Christ as their personal Savior so their names will be forever recorded in the *Lamb's Book of Life*, not because they deserve it, but simply because of God's mercy and grace.

"Thank you, Father, for Your love, Your mercy and grace. Lord, let me be an example and let me live so that they will always see your Holy Name glorified in my life."

Day Five

I will praise thee; for I am fearfully and wonderfully made: marvelous are thy works; and that my soul knoweth right well. Psalm 139:14 KJV

For all of Kelly's three years of life I had been working two jobs. Often she wanted to spend the night with me, but because my second job included night work, she was never allowed to stay. Eventually I was able to tell Kelly that I was quitting my second job and hoped to be back to normal soon. I continued to work for a few more weeks and I guess Kelly became impatient. One day she called and asked, "Granapple, are you a normal granapple yet?"

I had to laugh at her question but then I began to wonder just what is normal anyway? We are all one of God's original masterpieces made in His image. There is no one else exactly like me; no one with my personality or abilities. Some may not be perfect physically or even mentally, but God has a special place for us in His Kingdom. We are unique, one of a kind, and precious in His sight.

"Thank you, Lord, that You made us and You love us just the way we are. You have gifted each one of us for the special purposes You have in mind for our lives. Thank You that You have prepared our hearts to respond to You and live for Your glory. Help my grandchildren to know that from the time they were conceived they were unique and one of a kind because You made them special for Your glory."

Day Six

For by grace are ye saved through faith; and that not of yourselves; it is the gift of God: Not of works lest any man should boast. Ephesians   2:8-9 KJV

Brooke, Kelly, and their families were visiting me. Brooke and Kelly had seen the little park close by and decided it would be fun to walk there to play. Kelly's mother, knowing they were not familiar with the neighborhood, informed them they could not go alone because she was afraid they would get lost. In all innocence, Kelly replied, "Mother, you know if we get lost, we'd come tell you!"

We may smile at Kelly's lack of understanding of what lost means, but I wonder if we truly understand what it means to be spiritually lost. To be spiritually lost means that we will spend eternity in hell unless we repent and turn to God. Aren't we thankful for a God who stands willing to forgive and who loves us enough to give His only Son to pay the penalty for our sins?

"Thank you, Lord, for the gift of Your Son and for our salvation so we can know beyond a shadow of a doubt that we belong to You. Thank you that we can place our lives in Your hands and have the peace, and comfort that only You can give. Thank You for Your wonderful grace and the free gift of Your salvation. My prayer for my grandchildren is that they will accept You as their personal Savior at a very early age."

Day Seven

Whereby are given unto us exceeding great and precious promises: that by these ye might be partakers of the divine nature, having escaped the corruption that is in the world through lust. 2 Peter 1:4 KJV

A friend and I took the two grandsons to the air show, the biggest and best in the entire nation. It was fabulous! A special attraction was the sleek, black, stealth bomber that had played such an important part in the Gulf War. My friend and I were deeply impressed as we watched the daredevils performing their stunts. The boys were excited as we toured all the different kinds of airplanes on display. They were in awe of the parachute jumpers, the reenactment of a wartime battle, and the lady who walked on the wing of her plane. Later when Brian's father asked what he liked best about the air show, Brian replied without hesitation, "The hamburgers!"

I thought *how like that we are.* We settle for something less than the best in our lives and we miss the main events by concentrating on those things that bring temporary joy. Our vision of what we can be is never realized because we are content with sampling the "goodies" of life without ever tasting the "main event" God has in store for us.

"Lord, help my grandchildren to not settle for the temporary worldly pleasures, but instead seek the best in life as they prepare for the treasures You have prepared for them in heaven."

Day Eight

Call unto me, and I will answer thee, and shew thee great and mighty things, which thou knowest not. Jeremiah 33:3 KJV

An excited Jordan called long distance and without pausing for a breath shared with me this choice bit of information. "I saw a rattlesnake today; I got two baby kitties; the goose chased me; I fell out of the tree and got "hurted," and I learned to swim."

After picking myself up off the floor and offering words of comfort, I realized that Jordan's narrative is the story of our lives. Many times we see a rattlesnake or some sin that if touched would be fatal. Then just as Jordan's daddy killed the snake and shook the rattlers in Jordan's ear so he would know the sound of danger, hopefully, I hear and recognize the sound and sight of sin and run the other way. Sometimes I feel like a goose is chasing me when I am caught up with the cares of the world. It's then I have to do what Jordan did. He stopped, picked up a big stick, and chased the goose. That is when I have to pick up God's word and call on Him to rid my life of circumstances that make me feel like I am being chased. Just as Jordan surely treasured the moments with his warm, fluffy kittens, I treasure the moments when I feel the warm, refreshing presence of God and know again that He is in charge and all is right with my world. But then again, I fall every now and then and get "hurted" but God is always there to pick me up and put His arms around me and comfort me as I'm sure Jordan's mother did him. Then finally, like Jordan, I learn to swim when I listen to God's instructions and His voice through the circumstances He sends my way.

"Thank you God for your comfort and forgiveness when I fall and for Jordan and the lessons I learn from him about the love of God. May he always call on You when he gets 'hurted.'"

Brooke Johnson

Day Nine

Let your light so shine before men, that they may see your good works, and glorify your Father which is in heaven. Matthew 5:16 KJV

Once when four-year-old Brooke was spending the day with me, she painted a little plastic sun catcher.

"I made this for you, Granapple," she said.

Of course I thought it was beautiful even though the paint was a little smeared and one color ran into the other. After looking through the house for just the right place to hang it, Brooke excitedly exclaimed, "Let's hang it in your bedroom window so you'll see it every morning when you wake up." Amazingly, the little sun catcher looked beautiful with the sun shining through it. The smeared paint did not even show. Brooke was very pleased with her handiwork.

A few mornings later I woke up feeling depressed and discouraged over some problem I had to face that day. As I lay there for a minute dreading to get up, my eyes fell on the sun catcher. It looked dull and drab and all the imperfections showed. *That's just the way I feel today*, I thought as I slowly pulled myself out of bed. Then as I opened the shade, the little sun catcher seemed to come alive and was instantly transformed into the bright, shining object it had been when we hung it. What a difference a little sunshine had made and what a difference it makes in our lives when we allow the Son to shine through us. The little sun catcher lifted my spirits and I felt better the rest of the day.

"Lord, because of what You have done for us, my prayer is that my precious grandchildren will never fail to let Your light shine through them to show others the way to You."

Day Ten

Have I not commanded thee? Be strong and of a good courage; be not afraid, neither be thou dismayed; for the Lord thy God is with thee whithersoever thou goest. Joshua 1:9 KJV

Tornados in Oklahoma are quite common in the spring. Kelly was in first grade when a tornado warning was broadcast and everyone was warned to take cover. You can imagine how frightened she and the other children were as they huddled together under their desks as the tornado passed over. This experience left Kelly very afraid of storms.

Later during a severe thunderstorm, in trying to reassure her I recalled an incident we had experienced when her father was a small child. We were camped at the lake when an early spring storm came up unexpectedly. While we huddled in our tent listening to the howling wind and waiting for the driving rain to stop, we watched as our new boat, anchored nearby, slowly sank into the lake. The storm continued to rage all about us. The trees were nearly bent to the ground as the driving rain continued in all its fury. To take the children's minds off the storm, I called their attention to a little bird's nest fastened securely to one of the swaying tree branches. There in the nest was a little bird that appeared to be asleep. His head was tucked under his wings, and he was sitting perfectly calm as the storm worsened. As thunder roared and lightening flashed, the little bird felt perfectly safe because it knew that God was in control.

This was a perfect picture of peace in the midst of a storm. I explained to Kelly that God wants to give us the same peace and comfort that He gave that little bird. Kelly will probably never learn to enjoy the storms that will come her way throughout her life, but my prayer is that she will learn to enjoy God's presence in the midst of the storm.

"Thank you, Lord, for Your nearness in the times of fear and distress as we go through the storms in our lives."

Day Eleven

Be sober, be vigilant; because your adversary the devil, as a roaring lion, walketh about, seeking whom he may devour. 1 Peter 5:8 KJV

His Sunday School lesson that day had been about how Satan is roaming the earth and is ready to destroy us if we are not careful. As we were discussing how evil and deceptive Satan could be, the dog next door began barking. I realized that I was losing Jordan's attention as I continued to explain that we had to always be on guard against Satan.

Finally, he interrupted and asked, "Granapple, is Satan as mean as pit bulls?" That was the meanest thing he could think of.

What a chance for an object lesson! I went on to explain that Satan is far meaner and deceptive than a pit bull. Just as we have to be on guard when we are around pit bulls, we have to be on guard every minute of our lives against the wiles of Satan. The Bible says that Satan is like a roaring lion seeking whom he may devour. However, we can praise God that even though Satan is powerful, he cannot prevail against the blood of the Lamb and the name of the Lord Jesus Christ. Watch out for Satan and the pit bulls in your life!

"O God, help my grandchildren to know that they can always call on You when they are attacked by Satan and You are always there to comfort and deliver them."

Day Twelve

And we know that all things work together for good to them that love God, to them who are the called according to his purpose. Romans 8:28 KJV

Brian had fallen and scratched his knee. I quickly dispensed a kiss and a band aid. Attempting to take his mind off the hurt, I began to sing, "God can take our hurts, and this we all know. He mixes them all together in a beautiful rainbow." I'm not much of a singer and the words didn't rhyme very well or make much sense, but they did the trick. It was not long before Brian was singing with me and had forgotten his hurt.

I reminded Brian of the first rainbow that God gave to Noah as a reminder of good things to come in his life. I hope every time Brian and my other grandchildren see a rainbow they remember that good can come from hurt if we turn it all over to Him. God can take away our hurt and make us content and at peace in every circumstance in our lives and we can say with the Apostle Paul, "...I have learned to be content in all circumstances." (Philippians 4:11b) He does not always take us out of our bad circumstances, but He always goes through them with us.

"Thank you, Father, for Your love and care every day. I thank and praise You for the hurts and rainbows my precious grandchildren will experience in life. Even though the hurts may be painful and I would love to take those experiences away from them, I know that You will work all things together to grow them as Christians."

Day Thirteen

Lest Satan should get an advantage of us: for we are not ignorant of his devices. 2 Corinthians 2:11 KJV

One day Jordan was playing with a plastic sword. As I walked into the room, I saw him trying to hit the ceiling fan with his toy sword. It startled me and using my sternest voice, I scolded, "Jordan, do you know what would happen if you got that sword caught in the fan?"

His eyes widened as excitement grew and with anticipation in his voice, he came back with, "No, Granapple, what?"

I thought for a moment and then realizing I did not have a clue what would happen, I blurted out, "I don't know!" We both cracked up with laughter. The rest of the day was such a blessing as together we laughed at everything that happened.

As Jordan was probably flirting with danger by poking the sword into the fan, many times we flirt with danger when we do and say things we know we shouldn't do, go places we shouldn't go, and watch things we shouldn't watch on television. I realize as they grow up the dangers will be more prevalent and with greater consequences. It behooves me to make the most of the time I have now while they are small to teach my grandchildren about God. I must teach not only by word, but also by example.

"Oh God, let my precious grandchildren ever be mindful of the dangers of flirting with the things of Satan and keep their minds and bodies pure and clean for Your service. Help them to know they can always call on Your strength to help when tempted to flirt with the things of Satan."

Day Fourteen

For he shall give his angels charge over thee, to keep thee in all thy ways. Psalm 91:11 KJV

Jordan and Brooke's mother was in the hospital and I was staying with them for a few days. They had been promised two baby kittens by one of the neighbors, so they persuaded me to take them to get the kittens. We picked up the little kittens and returned home. As soon as the pickup door was opened, out scampered the kittens. Here came the dogs barking and took chase. Behind the dogs were Jordan and Brooke screaming at the dogs to leave the kittens alone. I didn't know what was going to happen, so I went running along behind. What a picture we must have made! Finally, the kittens ended up in the tree and Jordan climbed up to get the frightened creatures. They were safe as long as they were in Brooke and Jordan's arms, but they wanted their freedom. However, when given their freedom, they encountered danger from the dogs. Fighting off the dogs, we finally managed to get them safely in the barn.

How like the frightened kittens we are. It is when we choose our own way instead of staying in the safety of God's perfect will that we encounter Satan's traps and find ourselves in real danger.

"Father, keep my precious grandchildren in Your perfect will and safe from the pitfalls of sin, even if we have to climb a tree as the kittens did."

Day Fifteen

My little children, let us not love in word, neither in tongue; but in deed and in truth. 1 John 3:18 KJV

Grandchildren can bring you back to reality. One day as I was applying my makeup, I was complaining about looking old. After listening to me complain for a little while, four-year old Kelly came over, took my face in her little hands, looked directly in my eyes and said, "You're not old, Granapple, you just look that way."

Thanks a lot, Kelly! With Kelly around I will never get to thinking too highly of myself. As I thought about what she had said I began to wonder if I just look like a Christian because I am at church every time the door opens, or can Kelly see Christ in my life every day? Oh, I know I have not committed murder or some of the other so called "big sins," but have I been critical of someone, gossiped, hurt someone's feelings, or been too busy to help someone in need? And what about the sins of omission? Have I done everything God would have me do? Have I withheld my resources, both time and money, in order to further my own needs? Have I harbored pride or jealously in my heart?

"Oh Father, make me a good example for my grandchildren. Help them never have to wonder if I just look like a Christian; but help them to always know that I am a Christian because of my words and actions."

Day Sixteen

The Lord is merciful and gracious, slow to anger, and plenteous in mercy. He will not always chide: neither will he keep his anger forever. He hath not dealt with us after our sins; nor rewarded us according to our iniquities. Psalm 103:8-10 KJV

Brian was watching his father put together a swing set in their back yard. After he had witnessed a lot of sweat, strain, and groaning, he took his life into his own hands and crept up close to his father.

"Daddy, you must love me an awful lot," he said. His father said all his aggravation and tiredness left immediately. With just a few heart-felt words, Brian had made all the hard work worthwhile.

Sometimes we are so wrapped up in our own lives that we forget that there are others who need words of encouragement and love. Then we must never forget that our Heavenly Father longs to hear our words of appreciation and love for all that He does for us every day. As we fill our lives with worship and praise, God reveals Himself to us in new and unusual ways. May my precious grandchildren never forget that our chief goal in life is to worship and glorify God.

"Father, today I praise You for who You are, my Creator, my Savior, my God, my Sustainer. I praise You that You are compassionate and gracious, full of loving kindness, and always ready to forgive. I praise You that You are patiently considerate and generous beyond my imagination. May my grandchildren never forget to praise You just for who You are!"

Brian Koonce

Day Seventeen

I press toward the mark for the prize of the high calling of God in Christ Jesus. Philippians 3:14 KJV

Easter was a special time for Brian and Kelly when they came to my house for an Easter egg hunt. There was always a "prize" egg, which contained some little prize that made the hunt worthwhile for Kelly. This Easter I had forgotten the prize egg. After diligently hunting and not finding a prize egg, Kelly was plainly disappointed and she let us know that in no uncertain terms. The rest of the day she was out of sorts because she didn't get a prize.

In life we don't always get the prize, do we? Circumstances happen in our lives and we become discouraged and disappointed. On those days I am usually out of sorts and don't feel much like a Christian. However, I thank God my relationship with Him does not depend on my feelings or circumstances any particular day because feelings and circumstances have a way of changing. I am so thankful that my relationship with Him depends on His word and His word never changes.

"Thank you Lord, that I can always depend on the truths in Your Word. My prayer for my grandchildren is that they will strive for the ultimate prize in life, which is You! I pray they will live for You all the days of their lives no matter the circumstances."

Day Eighteen

Finally, my brethren, be strong in the Lord, and in the power of His might. Put on the whole armor of God, that you may be able to stand against the wiles of the devil. Ephesians 6:10-11 KJV

Jordan loves any creepy, crawly things. He was taking great delight telling me how his mother had recently killed a rattlesnake. He gave quite a dissertation on rattlesnakes, telling me how far the rattler can reach when it strikes, how rattlesnakes sound and various other things I didn't particularly want to know. He said that his daddy told him that if you can hear a rattlesnake you can kill it, but it's the ones that are not rattling that you should worry about.

Isn't that the way it is in life? We can combat the sins and temptations that are obvious, the ones we can see, but what about the silent ones, the ones that slip up on us like the sin of pride, jealousy, anger, and unforgivingness? What about the sins of omission? Sometimes they are worse than those of commission. When we accepted Christ as our Savior, we made a commitment to Him. Are we keeping that commitment? Are we molding our life to His?

"Dear Lord, today I pray for my grandchildren that their hearts will be strong and committed to You. May they always call on Your power and take advantage of the armor You have given them to use against Satan. May they be like You!"

Day Nineteen

A new heart also will I give you, and a new spirit will I put within you; and I will take away the stony heart out of your flesh and I will give you an heart of flesh. Ezekiel 36:26 KJV

One thing that Brooke loves to do when she visits me is for the two of us to make cookies. Mostly, I think she liked to play in the dough and I'm always game because I just love being with her. This day she was making all sorts of different things out of the dough.

Pretty soon she held up a piece of dough and exclaimed, "Look, Granapple, I made a heart."

I admired her heart and went on about my business. Brooke soon became bored with the heart so she took it and smashed it all together again. I watched as she played with it awhile, and then rolled it out again and voila – another heart!

"Look Granapple, I made me a new, better heart."

I thought as I watched Brooke *that is exactly what God does for us.* He takes our old stony heart of flesh and replaces it with a new heart and a new spirit when we confess our sins, repent, and humbly turn our lives over to Him.

"O God, my prayer is that You will give my grandchildren new, clean hearts as they confess their sins to You. Only You, Lord, can replace a cold, broken heart with a heart full of love and compassion for our fellow man."

Day Twenty

My little children, let us not love in word, neither in tongue; but in deed and in truth. 1 John 3:18 KJV

By the time Kelly was two years of age she had become quite a talker. Before she goes to bed each night she has a ritual that must be performed. After saying good night to the pictures of grandparents and cousins, she then gives her brother a hug and kiss. Finally it's Daddy's turn. On nights when she's not sleepy, she will walk around the room a long time saying, "I love you, Daddy," like a broken record without ever coming near him or even looking at him. He knows she's just practicing her words. But when she finally crawls into his lap with a hug and kiss, puts her arms around his neck, and says, "Daddy, I love you," then he knows she means it.

Far too many times when we tell God we love Him, it is really just following a routine and practicing our spiritual words. Only when we crawl into the center of His will and embrace His plan for us do we really mean it.

"Oh Holy God, help my grandchildren to always seek Your perfect will for their lives and let them live so there will never be a question of whether they mean it or not when they say 'I love you, Lord.'"

Day Twenty-One

It is God that girdeth me with strength and maketh my way perfect. Psalm 18:32 KJV

When the grandchildren come to spend the night with me, bedtime is our special time together. This is when we all crowd together in my bed and a lot of loving and laughing goes on. We read a story out of one of their books, turn the lights out, and then the fun begins. I tell them a story using one or all of them as the hero. The boys love those stories best that I tell about the two of them hiking in the Colorado Mountains. For some reason it always has to be Colorado and their sisters cannot go along because of the danger. The story is that they get lost and end up having to fight off the wild animals. The greater the imagination, the better they like it. Often, one of them will pick up at this point and add so much that it becomes their story. As they roam the mountainside, they are always confronted with lions, tigers, snakes, and every exotic animal imaginable. The story really gets exciting when Jordan and Brian manage to fight off these animals with their play knives and popguns. They always come out the victor.

If only it could always be so in their lives. We fight the devil's lions and tigers of some sort in our life every day, don't we? How do we fight these dangers? With God's help and in His strength, of course!

"Father, may my grandchildren know they can always call on your strength when faced with Satan's temptations and dangers."

Day Twenty-Two

Now no chastening for the present seemeth to be joyous, but grievous: nevertheless afterward it yieldeth the peaceable fruit of righteousness unto them which are exercised thereby. Hebrews 12:11 KJV

Brian was spending a few days on the farm with Jordan. They were warned several times not to go near the tail pond pit. The tail pond pit is a pond of water that is being recycled for farming. It is a very tempting place for two little boys, but it can also be a very dangerous place. As the morning went on, Jordan's mother realized it had been some time since she had heard the boys. After looking around the house and not finding them, she was afraid that curiosity had gotten the better of them and they had gone to the tail pond pit. She jumped in the pickup and sure enough, there they were having the time of their lives playing in the water and mud. After a severe scolding, they were told to ride or walk their bicycles back up the hill in the hot, sweltering, Oklahoma heat.

Jordan begged, "Can't we just put the bicycles in the pickup and ride back?" However, part of their punishment was to get their bicycles back up the hill in the 104-degree temperature with Jordan's mother driving slowly behind them to keep them from resting. More discipline would come later. Jordan and Brian learned a lesson that day. They learned that disobedience brings discipline.

Don't you find that so in your own life? Discipline is hard but aren't we thankful for the love and forgiveness that comes from our heavenly Father?

"Precious Lord, may my grandchildren learn early that even though God forgives their sins, they still have to endure the consequences. Teach them, O Lord, that discipline is a mark of Your love and, if rightly received, is extremely profitable."

Day Twenty-Three

Thou wilt keep him in perfect peace, whose mind is stayed on thee; because he trusteth in thee. Isaiah 26:3

When my grandchildren were small, I would hug them real tight and tell them I loved them so much I was going to squeeze them in two and keep one for me to love. During one visit, things were not going well for me and I guess Jordan could tell.

After watching me mutter to myself and slam things around, Jordan said, "Granapple, you can have one of those 'squeeze-me-in-two hugs' now if you want it." You bet I did!

When things seem to pile up on you, when you don't know what to do or where to turn, don't you sometimes want to ask God for one of those "squeeze-me-in-two" hugs? He's always there standing with His arms outstretched waiting for you to ask. He wants to hug you more than you want Him to. Isn't that a comforting thought?

"Father, help my precious grandchildren always know they can call on You and that You will answer and give them comfort and peace when things are not going well in their lives. Thank You for who You are: the great Comforter, Mighty God, and Prince of Peace."

Day Twenty-Four

Open thou mine eyes, that I may behold wondrous things out of thy law.
Psalm 119:18 KJV

Brooke went with me to run errands. I was very rushed and having spent more time at a particular stop than I had planned, I complained that the world would be a better place if people would just take the time to smell the roses.

As we were driving by the library, Brooke exclaimed, "Look, Granapple, there are some roses, let's stop and smell them."

We stopped and smelled the biggest rose we could find. I hurriedly grabbed Brooke's hand and started back to the car thinking of all I had to do that morning.

Not to be rushed, Brooke said, "Granapple, let's smell the roses on the next bush." This went on until we had smelled a rose on every rose bush along the sidewalk. She had taken me literally when I said to stop and smell the roses. What a joy to spend time with my precious granddaughter admiring God's beautiful world and what a lesson for me!

God tells us in many ways to stop and smell the roses. When the cares of the world pile upon us and we seem to be going under, He is always there to lead us beside the still waters to rest and calm our souls; in green pastures where He supplies our every need and in the paths of righteousness that we might be like Him. Thank you, Brooke, for reminding me to stop and smell the roses.

"Lord, help me lead my grandchildren to see the beauty of the world around them and recognize the beauty inside them as they give their hearts and lives to You."

Day Twenty-Five

Watch and pray, that ye enter not into temptation; the spirit indeed is willing, but the flesh is weak. Matthew 26:41 KJV

Kelly had been in the hospital with bronchitis and it was not a very pleasant experience for her. Now her brother was in the hospital with a severe case of asthma. Three-year-old Kelly walked into his room, looked around and announced in a loud voice, "I'm not staying, you know! Who's coming to get me?" She had had enough of hospitals!

Oh, if we could all be so definitive when it comes to sin. Often, we get into trouble because we dabble with and then are sucked into the things of the world. I hope Kelly and all my grandchildren will always be quick to say to the world, "I'm not staying, you know!" My prayer is that they will learn early that all they have to do is come to God in humble submission, admit that they are sinners, repent of their sins, and accept Jesus Christ as their personal Savior. God always accepts us as we are and sends the Holy Spirit to lead and guide us. What love!

"Father, help us always be aware of the sin that so easily besets us and stay close to You. May all my grandchildren say to the world's pleasure, 'I'm not staying, you know!'"

Day Twenty-Six

But they that wait upon the Lord shall renew their strength; they shall mount up with wings as eagles; they shall run, and not be weary; and they shall walk and not faint. Isaiah 40:31 KJV

Brian and I were watching a nature show on television. There on the edge of a mountain was a beautiful majestic bald eagle ready for flight. It was clear from the darkening clouds that a storm was approaching. The lightening streaked across the sky and thunder roared, but the eagle did not move. He sat watching the approaching storm. As the storm neared and increased in intensity, the wind pounded the tall trees until they almost touched the ground. Finally the storm struck in all its fury. Then with a mighty screech that made both Brian and me jump, the eagle took off flying directly into the heart of the storm.

"Did you see that, Granapple," Brian shouted, "the dumb bird flew directly into the storm. I'll bet he could have outrun it!"

I confessed I did not know much about eagles, but I did know that eagles can fly higher and faster using the strength and power of the windstorm than they can fly without it. I continued to explain that God wants this experience to take place in our lives. When the storms come in form of troubles and trials, instead of letting them pull us down and defeat us, we need to use the power and strength of the Lord to get through them.

"Precious Lord, may my grandchildren always remember to call on Your strength when they go through the storms of life. All they have to do is pray and call on Your name and You will lift them up with Your power out of the storms in their lives and help them soar like eagles."

Day Twenty-Seven

Notwithstanding in this rejoice not, that the spirits are subject unto you; but rather rejoice, because your names are written in heaven. Luke 10:20 KJV

For some reason Kelly decided she wanted to be called different names. She was Princess, Snow White, or almost anyone but Kelly. Today she walked into my house and informed me her name was Bnoah. I'd never heard the name Bnoah before and wondered where it had come from. After questioning we found she had gotten the name from a cartoon about Biblical characters. One of the dinosaurs had said, "My name be Noah." So Kelly wanted to be called Bnoah. I called her that until near the end of the day when it was time for her daddy to telephone. I was then told to call her Kelly because her daddy might not know her by the name Bnoah.

We never have to worry about whether our heavenly Father knows our correct name. We do have to worry about whether we will answer when He calls us. Have you answered His call and accepted His free gift of salvation? If not, He may be calling your name just now. Are you sure your name is written in the *Book of Life*?

"Father God, thank You that You know all about us. Thank You that by accepting You we can know beyond a shadow of a doubt that our correct name is written in the Book of Life and one day we will spend eternity with You."

Kelly Koonce

Day Twenty-Eight

Woe unto you, scribes and Pharisees, hypocrites! for ye pay tithe of mint and anise and cummin, and have omitted the weightier matters of the law, judgment, mercy, and faith; these ought ye to have done, and not to leave the other undone. Matthew 23:23

I was baby sitting with two-year old Brian, one-year old Jordan, and six-month old Brooke. We were on the patio when Jordan slipped and fell on the picnic table. I rushed to pick him up to see how badly he was hurt. He was bleeding profusely from the mouth area and crying loudly. Brooke was scared by all that was happening and joined Jordan in crying at the top of her lungs. As you can imagine I was in a panic. Brian had been watching quietly from the sidelines as our little drama unfolded. As I tried to calm the screaming Brooke and bleeding Jordan, Brian decided he wanted to get in on the excitement. Coming over to me, he stuck out his hip and said, "Granapple, my left hip hurts." My first thought was that I would make it hurt right there!

Later after we determined that Jordan's injury was not serious and Brooke had calmed down, I thought how Brian's remark is sometimes typical of us. We are so engrossed in our own needs and wants that we forget those out there who are dying and going to hell because we haven't fulfilled our calling as Christians.

"Heavenly Father, there is so much we leave undone. There are so many we could pray for, someone only we can lead to You, a class we could teach, or a hungry person we could feed. Help my grandchildren not to waste time here on this earth with unimportant things, but to seek and follow Your perfect will for their lives. Father, help them to realize the urgency of telling others about You instead of majoring on their own hurts and wants."

Day Twenty-Nine

God is my strength and power: and he maketh my way perfect. 2 Samuel 22:33 KJV

It was Mother's Day and Brooke and Jordan had brought me a beautiful bouquet of roses. We talked awhile about the beauty of the roses and the beautiful world God has made for us. The next day when we looked at the roses one of them was wilted and soon died. As I looked to see what the problem was, I noticed that the rose had a short stem and had not reached the water in the vase.

What a great time for an object lesson! I explained to Brooke and Jordan that by not reaching its life-giving source, the rose had wilted and died. I told them how like that rose we are when we fail to reach our source (Jesus Christ) by not praying, not being obedient, or not being faithful to His teachings. We become shriveled and ugly inside and like the rose, we eventually die. Christ is our life-giving source and we need constant contact with Him to keep our lives bright, fresh, and alive. Brooke and Jordan may not have understood what I was saying, but it surely meant a lot to me.

"O Great Jehovah God, if we would only realize the power that we have at our disposal simply by reaching for our daily life-giving source and letting You fill us with Your power!"

Day Thirty

By Him therefore let us offer the sacrifice of praise to God continually, that is, the fruit of our lips giving thanks to His name. Hebrews 13:15

Three-year old Brian and I were lying on a pallet in the back yard making shapes out of the clouds and contemplating the world around us.

"Granapple, did you know that a rolie polie has eyes?"

Funny until now, I had never given a thought as to whether or not rolie polies had eyes! As Brian picked up a rolie polie to give me a closer look, we talked about how God had created even these small creatures just as He had created us. Then I made another discovery. You can poke a hot dog wiener through the hole in the fence, especially if there is a dog on the other side helping you. I was discovering all sorts of things I did not know. Of course, I do not know how many hot dog wieners I will poke through a hole in the fence, or how many rolie polies I will stare in the eye, but it's nice to know I can if I want to, especially when the information comes from my precious grandson. That night when we knelt to pray, we thanked God for all the creatures in the world.

"God must be really big to have created everything in this whole wide world," Brian observed.

"Yes, Brian, God is really big and He deserves our worship and our praise," I replied. We spent the rest of the evening singing praises to God.

"Dear Heavenly Father, my prayer is that my grandchildren always be aware of how big You are. May they always be in awe of Your majesty, grace, and mercy. Help me to teach them by example that worshipping You is more than an emotional turn on. Worshipping is offering ourselves to God to be His servants and to do His will."

Day Thirty-One

But God commendeth His love toward us, in that, while we were yet sinners, Christ died for us. Romans 5:8

Jordan and Brooke were playing around at the table and spilled a glass of milk.

"I'm sorry, Granapple, that we made a mess," Jordan said.

I quickly reassured him, "That's alright, Jordan, this mess is easy to clean. Just don't ever mess up my heart; only God can clean that."

Jordan was thoughtful as he watched me get the bottle of cleanser and wipe up the mess he had made. Finally he said, "Granapple, does God use that same cleanser to clean up hearts?"

"No, Jordan," I replied. "Only the blood of Jesus can clean up our hearts." I continued to explain that just as that milk was out of control when he spilled it, sometimes our lives get out of control. We get involved in things we don't know how to get out of and we deserve to be punished. However, God loves us so much that He gave His only Son, Jesus Christ, to die on the cross to take the punishment we deserve. So the shed blood of Jesus cleans up the "mess" we make of our lives and all we have to do is accept Him. What an awesome thought that is! What love!

"Heavenly Father, may my grandchildren never forget that it took the shed blood of Your precious Son to clean up our "mess" and give us abundant life here and now and eternal life in the future. I pray that my grandchildren will grow up realizing the high cost of their salvation."

Brian Koonce, 26 years. Graduated from OBU in 2005 with a degree in Journalism and is working as a reporter for the Missouri Baptist Convention newspaper, "The Pathway." Being the youngest and newest member of the staff, receives all the traveling assignments which he loves and is an eager volunteer. He not only is privileged to visit and report on activities of churches in Missouri, but also travels to mission sites throughout the world, reporting and photographing missionary activities. Brian is also attending Midwestern Baptist Seminary, working for a Master's degree in Religious Education and Journalism.

Jordan Johnson, 25years. Graduated May 2006, from Texas Tech University and worked as Assistant Strength coach at University of Arkansas for a year. He moved to Mississippi with the Head Strength coach when he was hired by Mississippi. He now serves as Assistant Strength Coach at the University of Mississippi (Ole Miss). Jordan is also in graduate school working towards a degree in Health and Sports Science. Jordan is very active in weekly Bible study with football players and other athletes.

Brooke Johnson, 24 years. Brooke attended West Texas A&M for 2 years, but decided college was not for her. She is now living and working in Amarillo, Texas. She and her girlfriend just returned from a vacation in Paris. Brooke is active in her church and participates in their "English as a Second Language" class and participates in other mission activities of her church.

Kelly Koonce, 21 years. Kelly is a senior at OBU and her 4 years at OBU has been more than paid for with scholarships. She was a Merit scholar and recently received the Leadership award given to the rising senior who demonstrates the greatest leadership potential. Kelly has been offered a position at Christian Heritage School here in Oklahoma City when she graduates in May (and would live with me) but has recently been offered a scholarship to get her Master's Degree at Vanderbilt university. There she would major in International Education.

None of them are married and all are outstanding Christians. Praise God!